A+ books

SIMPLY**SCIENCE**

KU-112-889

The Simple Science of SOIL

Emily James

raintree

a Capstone company — publishers for children

Raintree is an imprint of Capstone Global Library Limited, a company incorporated in England and Wales having its registered office at 264 Banbury Road, Oxford, OX2 7DY – Registered company number: 6695582

www.raintree.co.uk
myorders@raintree.co.uk

Edited by Jaclyn Jaycox
Designed by Jenny Bergstrom
Original illustrations © Capstone Global Library Limited 2018
Picture research by Jo Miller
Production by Tori Abraham
Originated by Capstone Global Library Limited
Printed and bound in China

ISBN 978 1 4747 4352 5
21 20 19 18 17
10 9 8 7 6 5 4 3 2 1

British Library Cataloguing in Publication Data
A full catalogue record for this book is available from the British Library.

Acknowledgements
We would like to thank the following for permission to reproduce photographs: Shutterstock: Alexander Bark, 8-9, Antonov Roman, 16-17, dnaveh, 26-27, Dragon Images, 24-25, Drakuliren, 22-23, Elvan, 21, Fabio Lamanna, 10-11, fotoslaz, 28-29, GalapagosPhoto, cover, George Dolgikh, 14-15, LexRiver, 7, marcovarro, 18-19, MR.RAWIN TANPIN, 6, Nick Biemans, 20, Riccardo Arata, 12-13, showcake, 13 (inset), spiphotoone, 23 (inset), Sujalmages, 29 (inset), Suzanne Tucker, 4-5. Design elements: Shutterstock: diogoppr, xpixel

Every effort has been made to contact copyright holders of material reproduced in this book. Any omissions will be rectified in subsequent printings if notice is given to the publisher.

All the Internet addresses (URLs) given in this book were valid at the time of going to press. However, due to the dynamic nature of the Internet, some addresses may have changed, or sites may have changed or ceased to exist since publication. While the author and publisher regret any inconvenience this may cause readers, no responsibility for any such changes can be accepted by either the author or the publisher.

CONTENTS

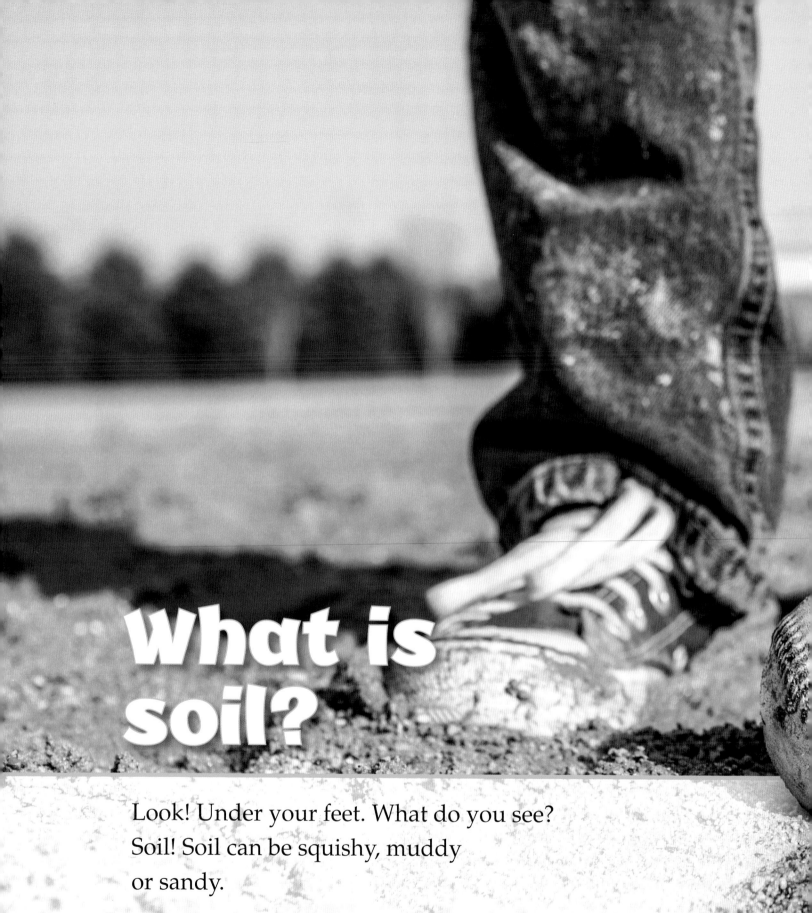

What is soil?

Look! Under your feet. What do you see?
Soil! Soil can be squishy, muddy
or sandy.

You can dig, play and plant flowers in it.
Soil covers almost all the land on Earth.
But what is soil?

Soil is a mix of different parts of nature.
Rocks form one part. Sand, silt and clay
are pieces of rock that make up soil.

Pieces of leaves and twigs also make up soil. So do tiny parts of animals that lived long ago.

Types of soil

Soil found near the sea is usually made of sand. Sand is mostly broken-down rocks and shells. It feels rough and gritty.

Sand has large grains. They do not stick together well. Water drains quickly through sandy soil. This soil does not have many nutrients. They are carried away by water.

silt

Silt is like sand. But silt's grains are smaller.
It is a dark colour. It feels soft and smooth.
Silt is a good soil for growing plants. It holds
a lot of food and water for plants.

Clay has even smaller grains than silt. It can be many colours. It feels soft and sticky. Clay does not drain well. Minerals stick to it. Minerals make clay a good soil for growing crops.

Humus is the dark, gooey part of soil.
It is made from rotting plants,
leaves, wood and animal matter.

Sticky humus helps hold the rocky parts of soil together. Humus contains food that plants need to grow.

Layers of soil

Humus, water and air are usually found in the upper layer of soil. This layer is called topsoil.

Topsoil is very dark and filled with
nutrients. It is the best soil for planting.
Topsoil can take hundreds of years to form.

topsoil

subsoil

solid rock layer

Under topsoil is subsoil. Minerals gather
in this layer. The roots of plants reach into
subsoil for food and water.

Deep below subsoil is solid rock.
No plants or animals live in this layer.
Soil forms from this rock.

Who lives in soil?

Millions of creatures live in soil. Beetles, millipedes and worms wriggle and crawl through it. Many decomposers are so small that you can't see them.

Decomposers make humus. They eat dead
plants and leave droppings in the soil.
The droppings are like vitamins for plants.

Animals can make soil better for plants. Snails, snakes and rabbits burrow into soil and loosen it.

They make holes that let air and water
reach the roots of thirsty plants.

What do we use soil for?

People use soil for many things.

Farmers use it to grow crops.

Engineers use it to build roads and dams.

Clay soil is used to build houses.
Sand is used to make cement.

How can we take care of soil?

Plant trees! Roots hold soil together.
Without trees, soil can be washed or blown
away. Leaves help protect soil from too much rain.

Don't litter! Rubbish can harm soil, plants and animals. Keeping soil healthy is good for all living things.

Soil keeps us alive. Without soil, plants cannot grow. Without plants, animals cannot eat. Without plants and animals, people would have no food.

Dig into soil. Pile it up and stomp it down. Plant flowers in it. Let it squish between your fingers and toes. See how amazing the world beneath you is!

Dig in!

Soil is all around us. It is in gardens and parks. It is beneath pavements and houses. Soil is not exactly the same everywhere. What is the soil made of where you live?

What you need:

shovel

white paper plate

What you do:

- Ask an adult to help you dig up one shovelful of soil. Make sure you dig down deep to get more than just the topsoil.
- Put the soil on the paper plate and spread it out.
- Look for leaves, sticks, bugs, worms and rocks. Make a list of all the things you find.

- Pour some water on the area where you dug up the soil. Does the ground hold a puddle for a long time? Or does the water sink right away? What does that tell you about your soil?

GLOSSARY

cement grey powder made from crushed limestone and clay

creature living being

decomposer living thing, such as fungi or bacteria, that feeds on dead plants and animals and turns them into soil

engineer person who uses science and maths to plan, design or build

grain very small piece of something

humus wet, dark part of soil that is made of rotted plants and animals; humus contains food that plants need

mineral material found in nature that is not an animal or a plant

nutrient something that is needed by people, animals and plants to stay healthy and strong

silt fine particles of soil that are carried along by flowing water and eventually settle to the bottom of a river or lake

FIND OUT MORE

BOOKS

Rocks and Soil (Moving Up With Science), Peter Riley (Franklin Watts, 2016)

Rocks and Soil (Popcorn: Science Corner), Alice Harman (Wayland, 2014)

Soil (Rock On!), Chris Oxlade (Raintree, 2016)

WEBSITES

www.bbc.co.uk/education/clips/z7rb4wx
Watch this video to learn about types of soil.

www.dkfindout.com/uk/animals-and-nature /earthworms-and-leeches/earthworms
Find out why earthworms are so important for soil.

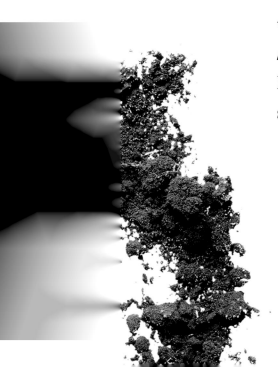

COMPREHENSION QUESTIONS

1. Soil found near the sea is usually sand. What is sand made of?
2. There are three layers of soil described. What are they?
3. Planting trees and not littering are two very important ways to take care of soil. What other things do you think you could do?

INDEX